In the Paint

In the Paint

Patrick Ewing
Linda L. Louis

Abbeville Kids
A Division of Abbeville Publishing Group
New York • London • Paris

This book is dedicated to my three children,
Randi, Corey, and Patrick, Jr., and to my late mother,
Dorothy, who encouraged my interest in art.
—Patrick Ewing

To my teachers, many of whom are disguised as my students.
—Linda L. Louis

Editor: Susan Costello
Designer: Celia Fuller
Production Editor: Owen Dugan
Production Director: Hope Koturo
Editorial Consultant: Joan Cear

First edition
10 9 8 7 6 5 4 3 2 1

Library of Congress Cataloging-in-Publication Data
Ewing, Patrick Aloysius, 1962–
    In the paint / by Patrick Ewing and Linda L. Louis.
      p.   cm.
    Summary: Describes the materials, techniques, and subjects for getting started in painting.
    ISBN 0-7892-0542-4
    1. Painting—Juvenile literature.   2. Child artists—Psychology—Juvenile literature. [1. Painting. 2. Art—Technique.]   I. Louis, Linda L.   II. Title.
ND1146.E84   1999
751—dc21   98-39255

Note to Adults

Tips for Parents and Teachers gives parents and teachers practical advice about how to support children as they find their artistic way: how to set up a painting space where children can work independently; how to help children get started and stay excited about their paintings; how to answer children's questions and respond to their work.

Contents

My Life In the Paint

by Patrick Ewing

What do YOU dream of being when you grow up?

When I was a boy, I never dreamed I'd be a professional basketball player. I lived on the island of Jamaica in the Caribbean. I never even played basketball until after I moved to the United States when I was 11. Even though I didn't dream of playing basketball when I was young, I did dream of doing a lot of other things. One of my dreams was to be an artist.

There were no art classes in my elementary school, but I drew and painted every chance I got. I remember sitting on the porch with my mother in Jamaica and drawing the characters in the comic strips in the newspaper. I felt great when she hung my drawings up in the house for my six brothers and sisters to see.

I kept drawing and painting after my family left Jamaica and moved to Massachusetts. That's when I started to play basketball. I used to shoot baskets after school with my friends. So you see, both basketball and art have been a part of my life for a very long time.

People are surprised to learn that I studied art in college. They don't know that when I wasn't on the court with the Georgetown Hoyas basketball team, I was painting and drawing. I enjoyed college— both the basketball and the studying. While I was at Georgetown, my team played in the National Collegiate Athletic Association (NCAA) finals three times and in my third year, we won the championship. That was a great feeling, but graduating from Georgetown University with a Fine Arts degree was even better because it fulfilled the dream my mother had for me before she died.

After I finished college in 1985, I was selected to play center for the New York Knicks. That's been my team ever since. During my basketball career, I've scored

◀ "My job as the Center for the New York Knickerbockers is to shoot baskets and pass the ball to my teammates."

a lot of points, earned a lot of awards and set a few records. But when all the pushing and shoving on the court are over and the fans have gone home, I go home, too, and sometimes I paint.

My fans are surprised to find out that I have an interest in art. Why not? I taught myself to draw before I taught myself to shoot baskets. Basketball is the side of me that everyone knows, but art is just as important to me. It's part of what makes me who I am.

I'll admit, I'm probably a better basketball player than I am an artist. I was never able to practice art as much as I wanted and, just like basketball, art takes lots of practice. But if things hadn't worked out in basketball, I might have tried to be a professional artist. Because

"When I'm out on the basketball court, I'm usually *in the paint.* Being in the paint means I'm playing in the painted part of the basketball court. The floor of the court is divided into different areas, the unpainted middle and the two painted circles under the baskets. The painted area near the basket is what I call my domain. I make my hardest decisions and most exciting moves when I am there—in the paint."

▲ "Recently I had my art on a credit card. Now fans have been asking me for paintings as well as autographs."

"I'm also _in the paint_ when I'm off the basketball court. I've loved to paint since I was your age. I like to paint landscapes or outdoor scenes from places I've been or pictures I've seen. I'm a visual person. I have to see something to paint it. Once I see it, I can mix different colors and put shapes together to show what I have in mind. That's the other way I like to be in the paint."

I enjoy both basketball and painting, I put my blood, sweat, and tears into both.

Since Discover® placed my art on a Private Issue® credit card, a lot more people have come to know me as an artist. Even my teammates have been asking for my paintings, because they think they will be valuable collector's items someday. But I don't paint to impress other people. I paint because I enjoy it and it makes me feel good.

I like to paint landscapes most of all. Sometimes I paint lush green mountains that remind me of Jamaica or quiet little ponds and tree-lined hills that remind me of places I've been on vacation. I like to paint from photographs, and sometimes I'll even take a picture of a place so that I can paint it when I get home. I'm a visual person, and I have to look at what I'm painting; I can't just paint from a picture in my mind.

Because art is such a strong influence in my life, this book is important to me.

With In the Paint, Linda Louis and I can show kids everywhere how to put their ideas on paper with paint. This book is also important to me because I have children of my own, and I know how much fun it is to spend time with them playing, working on a project, or making art. I like to cover a lampshade in my bedroom with drawings and paintings made by my daughter.

I would like to thank Linda for the good ideas, hard work, and creativity she brought to this book. I'd also like to thank Private Issue® for sponsoring this book and giving Linda and me a way to help children express their ideas and feelings with paint.

As a child on Jamaica, I never dreamed I'd be a basketball player, an artist, or even an author, and now I am all these things. What are you now? What are you in your dreams? I think we can all be artists and much, much more.

▲ "This is a real exciting part of the game so I showed the fans with blurry blue lines and the ball like it's on fire. The fans are clapping and standing and shouting all at once." **Julian**, eight years old.

Getting Started

Let's join Patrick *in the paint*.

It's a lot of fun exploring paint and discovering how to mix colors and use different brushes. Once you find out what paint can do, you'll be amazed at what you can do with it.

With this book you will understand how to turn your imagination, your ideas, and your feelings into paintings. You don't have to read the whole book at once. You can stop at any page and start again on another day.

On some days you will know exactly what you want to make. Other times you will get your idea from the surprising and unexpected things that happen while you are painting. It's all part of the fun.

Welcome, artists, let's get started.

Patrick Says "You'll see lots of paintings in this book that other kids have done. But don't think that there's only one way to paint something. Everyone's paintings will be different. You make the decisions about what to paint and how you will paint it."

Where is a good place to paint?

The first thing you need to do is to find a quiet place where you can set up your supplies, think about your ideas, and do your painting. You don't need a whole room, just a corner in your house or apartment where you can arrange things the way you want them. It's probably a good idea to ask an adult to okay the place you have found.

Look for a space where you can concentrate and not be distracted.

You will be using water, so it is easier if your painting place is near a sink.

It's best to work on a flat table, counter, or a deep shelf. You can even paint on the floor. Easels really aren't the best surface to paint on, because the colors might drip, and it is hard to mix your paints easily. So find a flat surface for painting.

Put newspapers down to protect your work surface—the table, counter, shelf, or floor.

It is important to have good light when you paint. Near a window is best, but any place with lots of light is fine.

Can you think of other places to paint? Kitchens, basements, porches.

Here's a supply list of everything you will need.

You can find many items on this list at home, but you will need to buy a few things from a store that sells art supplies.

An old cookie sheet, plastic lunch tray, or big Styrofoam meat tray that can hold five paint cups.

Five deep jar lids, or small plastic bowls, or furniture coasters, or cups to use as paint cups.

A small sponge or folded paper towel.

Three or four different sizes of paint brushes.

A clear plastic water container (a wide peanut butter jar is good).

BIG pieces of different kinds of paper to paint on. Heavy white drawing paper is good, and so are brown paper bags.

A stick of charcoal or chalk.

Tempera paint, which is sometimes called poster paint. It usually comes in a plastic bottle or small jug. The colors you need are red, blue, yellow, black, and white. **You'll soon see why you don't need orange, purple, or green paint.**

A stick to stir the paint in the bottle. Use something long (like a chopstick) and pour a small amount of each color in the paint cups, one color per cup.

How to arrange your supplies.

These pictures show you how to arrange your supplies. If you use your right hand to do things, put your tray on the right side of your paper. If you are a lefty, make sure your paint tray is to the left. Some artists like to stand when they paint, while others prefer to sit. Try both ways and do whatever feels right to you.

Patrick Says "Don't forget to wear old clothes or a smock so you won't worry about your clothes when you paint."

Start by choosing one of your brushes.

When you are ready to begin:

Hold your brush at the end of the handle so you can use your whole arm to paint.

Dip your brush into any color.

Wipe off the extra paint on the edge of the paint cup so it doesn't drip.

Now use this paint to make lines and shapes on your paper.

When you are ready to try another color:

Dip your brush in the water to clean it.

Scrub the bottom of the container until all the paint is out of the brush.

Then wipe your brush on the sponge.

Now you can dip your brush in a different color and paint new shapes, lines, or dots on your paper.

Washing and drying your brush carefully will help you keep your colors clean. Remember to wash your sponge and change the water after painting for a while.

Changing Paint

Be daring and try things you've never tried before.

If you haven't painted very much, get ready to discover what paint can do and what you can do **in the paint.** If you have already used paint, this part of the book will be a good warm up. Just like Patrick warms up before a game by stretching his muscles and shooting a few baskets, you need to warm up, too.

▲ "I can't explain it, but I've always loved the curvy roofs on buildings I see in Chinatown and it made me want to make those beautiful edges and colors in a painting. So I did." **Millie**, seven years old.

What is a good idea for a painting?

When you are learning to use your paints it's often better to paint a design than a picture of something. A design is a painting made up of shapes, colors, and lines that you arrange on the paper. When you make a design ask yourself, "Will the edges touch?" "Will the colors overlap?" "Will I put the same shapes on one side of the paper as the other?"

◀ **Philip**, nine years old, used all the colors on his tray to make his design.

It's fun to change paint by mixing colors.

Did you know that you can make many more colors from the ones you have in your paint cups? Put your black, white, and red paint off to the side for a minute and let's find out how.

Dip your brush in the blue. Instead of painting on the paper right away, place a dab of the blue on the tray. Then wash your brush and put a dab of yellow on the tray next to the blue. Now mix them together and watch what happens. What color did you get? How would the color change if you used more blue than yellow? Try it. Add even more blue. What happens? More yellow than blue? Try that too. If you start with yellow and then add blue, what happens?

▲ "I got the idea for this painting from my Dad's pictures of Vietnam. I mixed all different greens first and then decided where to put them."
Katie, ten years old.

Mystery question: Who else loves to use a lot of green in his paintings?
Clue: The answer is somewhere on page 8 or 9.

Are you ready to try mixing another color?

You just mixed blue with yellow and got green. What color do you think you will get when you mix red with yellow? Try adding different amounts of yellow to red and see what happens.

Patrick Says "Did you get one of the colors in my basketball jersey?"

▲ "It's midnight and the mountain lion is hunting for his dinner. I used more yellow than red because he is a golden kind of orange."
Joey, ten years old.

Wash the orange off your brush.

When you added yellow to red you got orange. This time you are going to add blue to red to get purple. Purple can be a tricky color to mix. Be patient and try different ways. You could start with red and keep adding little bits of blue until you get the purple you want.

▲ "This is my friend Teresa making a salad. Purple is one of her favorite colors."
Alison, eight years old.

Do you see why you need only red, blue, and yellow on your tray? Now you are thinking *in the paint.*

If you have these colors you can mix any other color you want. That's why these are called the "primary" colors. You can use the black and white to darken or lighten yellow, red, and blue, as well as the colors you mix.

Mystery question: Why is it important to keep the colors in your paint cups clean? **Clue:** Can you mix orange if there is blue in the yellow (turning it to green)?

◄ "First I covered the whole page with colors. Sometimes I mixed on the tray but mostly on the paper. Then I smooshed them around and put on some black dots."
Victoria, seven years old.

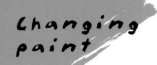
Practice makes you really good at mixing colors.

Patrick has fun at basketball practice because he can try new moves and improve his game. You can have fun at "paint practice" because knowing how to get the color you want lets you show your idea.

▲ "I put on blue and then when it was wet I put red over it and got purple. Then I did the orange, but I used red first, then yellow on top. It's a rainbow thunderstorm." **Julia,** seven years old.

▲ "The guy in the middle is floating in a design swimming pool of a million colors." **Nate,** nine years old.

A fun way to practice mixing is to paint the story of your day using only colors and shapes.

Think about your day so far. What woke you up this morning? A dream? An alarm? Your brother? What did you do then? Wash your face? Go back to bed? Trip over your sneakers? **Now decide how you want to show those things.**

▲ "I started with dark blue to show me sleeping. The red in the middle is the alarm clock. You can see what happened after that. I mixed an orange that is very bright and made lines on top of yellow to show me running around getting ready for school. Things calmed down after that, so I used different colors. It was really a good day after all." **Ally,** ten years old.

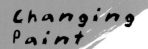

There are lots of ways to change thickness of paint.

Layering Just like putting a sweater over your tee shirt, you can put a layer of paint over another one. Try it. Mix a color and let a patch of it dry. Next, paint over it with a different color. Can you see any colors underneath? What happens if you paint over a color while it is still wet?

▲ "It was really cool to scratch through the paint and find another color underneath." **Sara,** eight years old.

Patrick Says "One of the best things about painting is that you can't make a mistake because you can always change things. If you don't like something you made on your paper you can paint over it, or you can turn the part you don't like into something else."

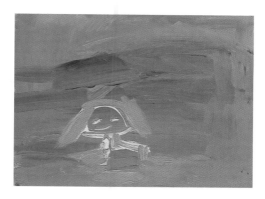

▲ "I am under water."
Narrah, eight years old.

Mix paint with water. Put some paint on your tray with your brush, and then mix it with water. Now paint a shape on your paper with this mixture of color and water. Can you see through it?

Paint over wet paper. Try spreading a little water on the paper with a clean brush and paint a shape on that wet area. What happens to the edges of your shape when you paint over wet paper?

Use no water at all.

Find ways to use paint as thick as you can. Try putting layers of paint on the paper using a completely dry brush. What other ways can you make your paint thicker?

▶ "This is a scene from the book *Misty of Chincoteague* when Paul, the Phantom, and Misty get caught in a whirlpool. All the layers of blue and white helped me to show the dangerous current."
Madeline, ten years old.

Using Your Brushes

Just as Patrick can use a variety of moves to score a basket, you can use different moves with your brush.

If you have been using a fat brush, try a skinny one now. You will see that a brush that is flat at the end or pointy will make different marks. Try pushing the brush, or dragging it, or twisting and rolling it. It's really fun to hold the brush by the bristles, spread them, and paint several marks at once. You may need to wash your hands after that last experiment.

Take your time and make your brush strokes slowly. Then see how the marks change when you do them fast.

▲ "This is a twister pulling a man and a bull into it. I was moving the brush fast when I painted this." **Clifford,** eight years old.

▲ "The best one is where I rolled the brush with two different colors on it. Can you find it?" **Anna,** eight years old.

Different brushes make different marks. Using the same brush differently makes different marks.

▲ "The snow was really deep so I dried the brush and used lots of white paint. It was a blizzard and we couldn't get the car out for two days." **Sam**, nine years old.

Some of your marks may look smooth, others may seem rough to you. Artists use the word, "texture," to describe the surface of the marks they make. Experiment by using different thicknesses of paint and different brush strokes. What textures can you make? Bumpy? Prickly? Slimy? Scaly? Think of as many textures as you can and try them all.

Patrick Says "When I paint landscapes of my favorite places, I use different brushes to make texture for the trees and water."

Different kinds of marks you can make.

Line Dip your brush in any color and try dragging the paint across the paper. Can you make a line that starts thin and gets thick by changing how hard you press? Try a line that loops back on itself, or a zig-zag line.

▲ "This is me. See, I'm walking my dog Sheba in the rain. Here's the umbrella." **Nitayja,** seven years old.

Dots While you were exploring lines you may have discovered another kind of mark, the dot. Try making big, bold dots by pressing hard with your brush. Now try making really tiny ones by just barely touching the paper with the tip of your brush. See how different dots look when you make them with the side of your brush. Can you make a line with just dots?

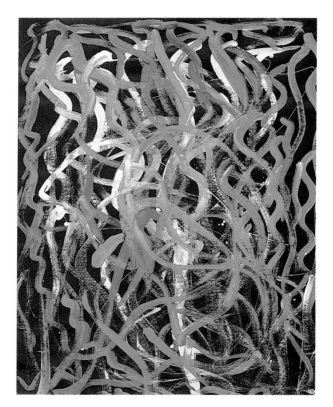

▲ **Brittany,** nine years old, pushed and pulled her brush all over the paper and made piles of lines.

Shape One of the best things about paint is how easily it spreads into the shape you want to make. Wash your brush, wipe it on the sponge to dry, and dip your brush in another color. Try turning two lines into a shape by connecting them and then filling it in. Now try making a shape without outlining it first.

▲ "This is the scene in the book where Black Beauty imagines the three friends are all together again. Even though Ginger is really dead I think it is a happy moment."
Coco, eight years old.

Practice some of the ways you have learned to change the paint and use your brush.

You could make a design using your imagination . . .

- - - - - - - - - - - - - - - - - ➤

Count how many times Zach changed blue.

▶ "I started with this leaf I made. Then I put it sticking up and the design inside was like teeth in a head. Then I started mixing blues to put it somewhere. See all the blues? I call it false teeth."
Zach, eight years old.

. . . or, you may decide to paint something that really happened.

◄ - - - - - - - - - - - - - - - - -

Natasha spread her paint in thick and thin layers.

◀ "I went to Africa with my two grandmas, my sister, and my mother. I painted the yellow this way because the sun was really, really hot."
Natasha, eight years old.

You may wish to use charcoal first to map out your painting.

If you want to plan your painting before you start, you can use a piece of charcoal to do it. Sometimes when you use pencil instead of a piece of charcoal you make a great **drawing**, but it's too small to paint. Paintings and drawings are different. When you **paint** you want to think about shapes and areas of color, so use charcoal to show your idea as big as possible.

▶ "It took a really long time but I'm glad I lined up all those square dots to show the windows in the Empire State Building. I drew charcoal lines first to make sure everything is straight." **Adam**, nine years old.

Patrick Says   "Whether it's basketball or painting, practice lets you come up with your own way of doing things. It shows you what you're good at and makes you better at the things you need to work on."

Painting Yourself and Others

To paint yourself, your friends, and your family you will need to mix colors to match their skin as closely as possible. That means you must learn to mix brown, because we are all different mixtures of browns.

▲ "It's a sleep-over birthday party." **Zoe,** ten years old.

If the colors you made in your practice paintings got mixed together, you have probably discovered how to mix a brown.

Think about how you made green, purple, and orange. You combined two different primary colors (red, blue, and yellow). Now mix all three together.

Now that you know how to mix brown you can make a color close to yours. **See for yourself.**

To make brown, you mix red, blue, and yellow all together.

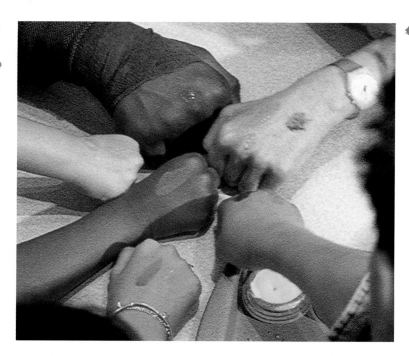

Mystery question: Whose hand do you think this is in the middle?
Clue: He loves being "in the paint."

▲ Put a dab of one of the browns you just mixed on the back of your hand. What do you need to add to make it a close match to your skin color? Are you lighter or darker? Redder or bluer? Maybe you need to add green. Try different mixtures until you closely match your skin color.

Let's help Patrick's friends match their own skin colors.

Use your sponge to make a clean area on your tray, and make sure all your cups of primary colors (red, blue, and yellow) are full. Now you are ready to mix skin colors.

Jasmine mixed brown the hard way. She started with blue, added a little yellow and black, and got a muddy green. Then she added some red, and that got her closer to the kind of brown she is.

Sergio mixed red, yellow, and blue and got brown right away. He added a little more yellow, red, and a touch of white.

Hannah first tried pink (white and red) and a little yellow. This didn't match, so she added some purple she had on her tray. This made it much closer, because by adding purple she added the missing primary color (blue) she needed to make brown.

▶ **Cathy,** eight years old, has shown two friends playing checkers.

▲ "I am sitting at the art table."
Neeahsha, eight years old.

▲ "This is my Dad."
Ciaran, eight years old.

Practice mixing skin colors by painting yourself, your family, or your friends doing something you really like to do.

▲ "This is a self-portrait, but I didn't try to make it look just like me. I wanted it kind of abstract." **Andrea,** ten years old.

▲ "This is me walking in the nature preserve without any grown-ups. My cousin is there, but you can't see her." **Nora,** eight years old.

Remember to start by mixing red, blue, and yellow to make brown. Then change the brown by adding another color or two to match the people in your painting.

Think about the things you do in your own life.

Who do you know best? Where have you been lately? What would you do if you could do anything you want?

▲ "This is my Grandpa Joe drinking yellow lemonade." **Miles,** nine years old.

Patrick Says "I like to take photos when I go on vacation with my family so I can remember the details later that I want to put in my painting."

◄ "This is my brother Steven in front of the window in our living room."
Olivia, nine years old.

▲ "I painted my Mom and my dog, Kenny. I made the corner where his bowl is dark because it's a shadow."
Taku, nine years old.

◄ "After school I like to skateboard. There's a skate park in my neighborhood. It's by the river."
Ernesto, eight years old.

Showing Your Ideas

Now try using colors, shapes, and textures to show your own ideas, feelings, and daydreams.

Artists like to paint familiar things—the people they know, the places they've visited. They also use their imaginations and paint things as they might be.

▲ **Anna,** eight years old, is pretending to be a leaf falling past a flock of birds who are flying away from a huge fire in the sky.

Patrick Says "Never stop exploring. Stay *in the paint* and let your idea take shape as you go."

Show your own point of view in your ideas.

Your paintings will be different from the ones you see on the next few pages. That's because your experiences are different from those of the kids who made the paintings.

From a distance (as if you were looking through a camera) . . .

▲ "This is me, my friend, her Dad, and some ladies at the hairdressers. I am getting my hair braided and my friend is getting hers curled." **Abeje,** eight years old.

. . . or, paint a close-up of a scene (as if you were in the painting).

▲ "This painting of the archery target is so close up that my arm's in it. The green is the grass behind everything." **Ali,** seven years old.

You could ask yourself,
"How do I get to school in the morning?"

Some of you walk to school in your neighborhood, and some ride the bus to a school in another town. Maybe you live away from home at a boarding school, or maybe you are schooled at home.

▲ "I walk my dog Inky to school. My Mom is with me and there's a taxi on the street." **Hannah,** eight years old.

Patrick Says "Even if you and a friend walk to school together, your paintings will be different because you see differently and remember different things."

You could paint the way you really get to school or choose one of these ideas and paint it your own way.

▲ **Ryan,** seven years old, is riding his bike in the school parking lot.

What part of your trip to school will you show?

What do you pass? Trees in the forest? City buildings?

If you take the school bus, where does it stop to pick you up?

Do you carry your books and other things in a backpack?

Does someone drive you to school?

Do you ride your bike to school? Are there any steep hills to climb on the way?

Will you show yourself in your painting?

If you'd like to paint about getting to school, you could ask yourself these questions.

- What colors do you need to mix to show the way to school?

- Will you layer colors on top of one another?

- What lines and shapes will you use to show the important places you pass on your route?

- How can you change the paint to show the textures of different places along the way?

▲ "This is me pretending to drive my car going speedy fast. The friction was making sparks come up, and the brakes were starting to go on the ground." **Andrew,** seven years old.

▲ "I am tripping on my shoelace and falling down the stairs on my way to school. I was all right." **Pedro,** nine years old.

Think now about getting started.

How you will position your paper? Do you have a tall idea or a wide idea?

Will you draw your idea first lightly in charcoal? Or will you start by mixing colors and putting them on your paper?

Will you start with what is in front or in the background? The biggest things or the smallest?

▲ "This is me pretending to get to school by boat. You can see me through the sail, because I made the paint really thin. I'm really not out there alone."
Micah, eight years old.

You could ask yourself,
"What fierce or friendly animals do I know or can I imagine?"

▲ "Bats live in caves. They are fierce to their enemies and friendly to their babies." **Richard**, eight years old.

▲ "Ann is leading Black Beauty back to the stable. She is black and courageous and has a white star on her forehead." **Lily**, nine years old.

◀ **Miranda**, eight years old, has shown two deer in the field with air in between the sky and the grass.

Before you start painting, think about what makes an animal fierce or friendly.

What animals can you name that are usually friendly? Puppies? Dolphins?

Can wild animals like deer be friendly?

How do animals show you that they are fierce or friendly? Rub up against your leg? Make a noise to warn you away? Show their claws?

Can friendly animals sometimes be fierce? When?

Where does your animal sleep? In a nest? On your bed? In the laundry basket?

▲ "Here's a tiger really close up. Mostly they are fierce, except when they are cubs."
David, seven years old.

▶ "This is me with my pet rat, Igor. People think that rats are bad, but he's a good one."
Milo, eight years old.

Now that you have a picture in your mind, let your colors, shapes, and brush strokes give you more ideas about how to paint your animal.

▲ **Hannah,** nine years old, is holding her breath as she dives under the water with a dolphin.

Will you use your brush a special way to show your animal's fur or feathers?

How can you arrange shapes to show what your animal is doing? Is it running, leaping, or sleeping?

If your animal lives in the water, how will you change the paint to show its wet home?

If your animal lives in the forest, what colors and shapes will show that?

Patrick Says

"Like me, you can paint what you feel like painting. I paint because I enjoy it, and it makes me feel good."

Follow your idea as you begin to get
in the paint.

▲ "This is my turtle eating his dinner in the sunset." **Harry,** seven years old.

Will you start painting the animal first or a place where your animal could be?

Will you show your animal from the front? A side view? Maybe from the back?

Mix colors on your tray or right on the paper. It's your choice.

What point of view will you show? A close-up? Long distance?

Ask yourself,
"What do people do in a group?"

✔ Patrick plays basketball and travels on an airplane with the team. What do you do with your family or a group of friends?

✔ Do you play a sport? If you do, where do you play? Inside or outside?

✔ Where did you go on your last school trip? Was the group mostly boys? Girls?

✔ Are the people in the group wearing special clothes? Uniforms? Are they dressed up? In swim suits?

▲ "The crowd is waiting to see if the player will dunk it. I made the lights shining down to show something exciting was happening." **Alex,** ten years old.

Do you want to show a group you really know or an experience that you imagine?

▲ "This is a view from the inside of my Mom's coffee shop. The little girl is trying to get up on her stool, and it's snowing outside." **Annie**, nine years old.

Pretend you are in a shopping area, a busy train station, or singing in a chorus. Who is standing next to you?

What do you do with your friends on weekends?

What does it feel like to be in a crowd?

Where do you wait in line? The movies?

Are you part of the group or are you watching the group?

Let's look at Simon's decisions.

▲ "I showed the referee calling a foul. They almost made a goal."
Simon, ten years old.

Imagine you are playing in this soccer game. Is it an exciting moment? How do you know?

Simon put the referee in the center of his painting. What do you think is happening?

He used brush strokes that feel exciting. How do his figures also show the action?

How has he darkened and lightened colors to show near and far?

Simon's decision to show the game from above and the players from the side really works.

Kathryn made some choices about what to show.

▲ "This is a wedding, no special one. You are supposed to be at the back of the church." **Kathryn**, ten years old.

If you have been to a wedding, do you know what part of the ceremony Kathryn is showing?

Kathryn's painting makes you feel as if you are actually there. Where are you sitting if you have this view?

What do you know about the figures from the colors she chose?

Like Simon, Kathryn painted the background figures smaller. She also uses the line made by the edge of the benches to draw your eye to the back of the church.

Now think about your own idea and ask yourself these questions to help you plan your painting.

▲ "I made these guys skateboarding." **Gage,** ten years old.

- What shapes do you need to show the action?

- How will you arrange people's arms and legs if they are standing? Sitting? Dancing? Walking up stairs?

- Do you need specific colors for certain people or places?

- Will you thin paint for a reason? Layer it?

- Do you need to make a particular texture? If so, what brush will you use and how will you use it?

- Will you start with the people or the place?

More fun in the Paint

This may be the end of this book, but your fun *in the paint* is just beginning. You have a place to work and you know what materials you need. Keep exploring paint on your own. The more you use paint, the more discoveries you will make about what you can do with it.

All you need is practice. It's up to you. That's the fun part.

▲ **Terence**, seven years old, mixed blues to show a giant wave with older boys surfing on it.

Patrick Says "Here are some fun painting ideas, but you can think of lots more on your own. Goodbye for now."

More Ideas for Pictures

- What kinds of things do you do in your sneakers?
- How do you like to cool off on a hot day? What did you get better at over the summer?
- What exciting thing happened this year?
- What do you like to do by yourself?
- Where do you play with two or more friends?
- What kinds of jobs do mothers have? Fathers?
- What kinds of ways can you go places?
- What does it feel like to be wading in a brook? Or standing on the roof of a tall building?

Tips for Parents and Teachers

by Linda L. Louis

As a parent or a teacher, you may be reluctant to paint with children at home or in the classroom because you worry you are not "artistic." This is an understandable concern. Chances are most of you didn't paint much when you were growing up. Perhaps there was no art teacher at school, or if there was, no sink in the classroom to make painting possible. Maybe you did paint as a child but gave it up after a certain age. Whatever the reason, if assuming the role of art teacher makes you uneasy, you may be relieved to learn that no one can teach children how to paint, only how to be *in the paint*. By following the advice given here, I hope you will find painting with children a rewarding experience.

When you are helping kids it is important to understand that they have different artistic intentions than older adolescents or adults. Like adults, they change and manipulate paint in order to shape an idea or capture a feeling. However, school-aged children are less concerned with the formal aspects of art than mature artists. Their primary motivation is to tell a story or show an event about their own lives.

Once you realize this, it is easier to know what to do and say to support a child. Consider this painting by eight-year-old Erica that shows what I mean. To

Erica's painting of a wave

▲ "In the summer I swam everyday in the ocean and the waves were awesome like this one."
Erica, eight years old.

make her painting, Erica associated properties of paint with her experience of being caught up in the powerful curl of a wave. Erica was exploring what she could do with paint—that is, what colors, shapes, and texture she wanted to show. She made a connection between the color she had mixed, the movement of her brush strokes, and her memory of playing in the surf the previous summer. Her blue-green marks not only look like a wave but they capture the feeling of being in the wave.

There is no formula that will teach children how to match something *in the paint* with something in the world. This understanding emerges from encounters with the material. They must discover how to capture an idea with a color or brush stroke by exploring the paint and inventing solutions on their own. However, there is much you can do behind the scenes to help children feel comfortable about making these kinds of discoveries.

It is not necessary to read through this section from start to finish. You can refer to different topics as you need more information. I have divided this section into four topics: "Nuts and Bolts" gives practical advice about materials and procedures. "Helping Out" provides pointers on how to support without taking over. "Shaping Ideas" describes a method for helping children focus on their own experience. Finally, "Talking with Kids" suggests the language you can use to encourage and inspire them.

Nuts and Bolts

The painting space.

For many adults, being *in the paint* translates into being in charge of the paint, either at home or in the classroom. However, if you use common sense about storage systems, routines, and clean-up procedures, young painters can be relatively independent and take care of the space themselves.

Here are some tips that will allow you to spend less time cleaning up after your children, and more time observing and enjoying a side of them that you may never have seen before.

Setting up a work space.

It takes concentration for children to get their ideas down in paint on a piece of paper. They need an area to work in that is free of distractions, where they do not have to hunt for supplies or clear off a space to work. Try to locate the painting place in an open, lightly trafficked area near a sink.

▶ Since there are bound to be a few accidents, choose an uncarpeted place to paint, with easy-to-clean surfaces that can tolerate standing water. If the weather permits, painting outside or on a porch is a terrific option.
▶ If the painting surface is not large enough or smooth enough to paint on, put a piece of Formica or well sanded wood on top. A 3-foot-by-4-foot (.9 m-by-1.2 m) surface will accommodate the paint set-up and a good-sized piece of paper. You can store the surface in a closet, in the basement, or behind a chest of drawers.

Supplies and Equipment

Many household items can be used for painting.

▶ Paint tray—A large Styrofoam meat tray will do, but a non-breakable plate or baking sheet is more stable and durable. It should be big enough to hold five small paint cups with empty space for mixing color (10-by-15 in. [25-by-38 cm] is ideal).

It is best if the tray has a lip or edge, has not been treated with a non-stick coating, and is made of a durable, non-rusting material, as it will be washed many times.

▶ **Paint cups**—Deep furniture coasters or jar lids are nonbreakable and hold about two ounces of paint. They can be stacked and stored inside a sealed plastic container so you don't have to wash them after each painting session.

▶ **Water containers**—A clear plastic container allows beginning painters to see how the water changes colors as they clean their brushes. A container with a wider bottom than top is most stable.

▶ **A small sponge** or a folded paper towel.

▶ **Paper**—Heavy, good sized, brown grocery bags or white department store shopping bags (18-by-24 in. [46 cm-by-61 cm]) so children can work large and layer paint. Cut up the bags into large, flat pieces.

Some things must be purchased from a store that has art supplies.

▶ **Paper**—If you buy paper by the sheet, make sure it is thick enough to stand up to many layers of paint (at least a 60 lb. weight [90 gsm]). Or you can buy rolls of white butcher paper and cut pieces to size.

▶ **Brushes**—Several good quality, long-handled, synthetic bristle brushes that are firm but not stiff, of varying widths (1 in. to ¼ in. [2.4 cm to 6 cm]) and shapes (flat and round). You don't need expensive natural or animal hair brushes, but don't get inexpensive ones either or the bristles will fall out. Wash them with warm (not hot) water and soap. Store them bristle end up.

▶ **Paint**—Non toxic, water-based, liquid tempera paint in red, blue, yellow, black, and white. Sometimes called poster paint, it comes in plastic jars or jugs and should be stirred before use to the consistency of heavy cream. It is handy to have a bit of turquoise paint on hand as it makes brilliant greens and purples.

▶ **Charcoal**—In case children want to "map out" their painting first. Children will want to use pencil, but discourage this because they are likely to draw something too detailed to paint with a brush. Coax children to use charcoal instead of a pencil.

Helping Out

Encourage discovery.

Great paintings are the result of choices artists make about how to change and use paint to capture their ideas and feelings. It may seem obvious to you, but children may need help understanding that before they can make paint do what they want they must find out what paint itself can do.

One of the most helpful things you can do for beginners or children with limited experience is to make sure they have time to explore the materials. Nothing ensures success more than confidence and skill in wielding paint itself. So encourage them to put time and energy into exploring paint.

Emphasize the process, not the result.

Show young artists you value the process as much as the product by not being overly interested in the image. Instead of commenting exclusively on the imagery, point out how colors or brush strokes

contributed to the success of the painting. For example, while reacting to his basketball figures, you
might say to Julian (page 10), "the way your blue
dots show the roaring fans really helps me understand how exciting this moment in the game is."

The paint tray.
A horizontal set up makes it easier for children
to manage their materials and encourages them
to mix colors (see page 14). Unlike an easel, the
tray serves as both a place to hold and mix paint.
At first, children may need help organizing their
actions in relation to the paint, tray, and brush.
Learn the simple routine outlined on pages 14–20
along with them, and you will appreciate how sat-
isfying it is for beginning painters to control their
own materials. Mixing color can be its own reward.
It is very common for young children to become so
absorbed in mixing colors that they never move
their greens and purples off the tray onto the paper.
This is a good sign, an indication that they are
completely involved and absorbed in thought.

Changing paint by mixing color.
No matter what age, beginners can become over-
whelmed if they have too many colors from which
to choose. At first, limit the paint tray to just two
primary colors (red, blue, or yellow) that make a
secondary color (green, orange, and purple). Do
this also with black and white until they become
confident (see pages 18–21).

For technical reasons that have to do with the
chemical composition of tempera paint itself,
purple can be tricky to mix. Help children figure

out for themselves that they must adjust the
proportions of red and blue until they get the
desired color.

The "story of your day" exercise will intrigue nine-
and ten-year-olds (see page 23). However, this
exercise may confuse younger children who do not
necessarily assign expressive qualities to colors.

It is easy to mix brown by accident, but children
may need some guidance when they first try to mix
it deliberately. Brown is made by mixing red, blue,
and yellow (the proportions will vary with the
brand of paint). If children ask you how to
mix brown, respond with a question that will help
them see that they must adjust the proportions (see
page 32–35). Look at their tray and see what colors
they have already mixed, staying away from colors
that have white or black in them. If there is a brown-
ish color ask, "How did you accidentally mix brown
here?" If they do not remember, or if there is no
color near brown on the tray, point to a secondary
color and ask them to recall what two colors are
already in that color. Ask, "What do you think will
happen if you add red to green (the color that is not
already in green), or yellow to purple?" This will
guide them to discover for themselves that all three
primary colors (red, blue, yellow) make brown.

Changing paint with a brush or water.
Children can move through pages 26 to 30 at
their own pace, but encourage them to explore
each concept thoughtfully. Younger children and
beginners will find it appealing simply to try out
various brushes and different ways to vary the thick-

ness of paint. Older or more experienced painters may need a bit of a challenge to stay involved in these simple explorations. You might suggest: "Can you make ten different kinds of lines with the same brush?" or "How could someone else guess which layer of paint you put on first?"

Overlapping.

Seven- and eight-year-old children rarely overlap objects in their paintings. They do not fully understand the concept of the paper as a picture plane, so they work out spatial relation-ships on the surface. It does not make sense to them that two different objects could occupy the same space on the paper. As a result, they line up people and animals (see pages 30 [below] and 46 [bottom left]). Whenever they do overlap, they must have a compelling reason to do so (see pages 41 [left], 45). One of the great joys of being in the paint with children is to watch how they first use inventions (see pages 32, 38, 52), and then conventions (see pages 10, 37 [right], 53), to solve the dilemma of representing three-dimensional space on a two-dimensional piece of paper.

White space.

Young children often leave white space between the sky and the ground in their paintings (see pages 28 [right], 45, 46 [bottom left, right). This is because they are more interested in depicting what they experience than representing what they actually see. Their experience of the world is that the sky is up, the ground is down, and "air" is in between.

Shaping Ideas

Getting started.

The question, "What should I make?" is a difficult one to answer. When children say they don't know what to paint, they often mean they are over-whelmed by the infinite number of possibilities. This section suggests four steps you can follow to help children see their own experience as raw material for their paintings.

Step #1:
Help a child focus.

You can help children get ideas by asking a leading question that focuses their thinking on meaningful events (see pages 42, 46, 50). Children are more likely to become involved and stay engaged in a painting if the subject matter is personally interesting and relevant to them. No matter how well-intentioned, adults do a disservice to young painters when they assign a topic or give them an activity book. Children will not become independent painters if they depend on you for ideas about what to make. Here are some age-appropriate questions:

Younger children.
► Where were you when you lost your last tooth?
► What games do you play when you are alone or with two or more friends?
► What kinds of things do you do on the weekend?
► What do you do to stay cool in the summer?

Older children.

▶ What kinds of things do you do in your sneakers? Or on one foot?

▶ What excitement have you seen on the street?

▶ What kinds of jobs do people have?

▶ What did you get better at over the summer?

▶ What is the first thing you do in the morning? Or the last thing at night?

Step #2:
Help them identify details.

Ask more questions to help them recall the particulars of the experience they are painting (see pages 43, 47, 51). Questions should be phrased so as to help children explore possible scenarios, clarify their ideas, and think about the details that will show their ideas. The point of asking these questions is not to get them to decide what to paint (although the subject matter may find its way into the painting). The purpose is to help them think about their own experience, so they can sort through what matters to them personally.

Step #3:
Help them think in paint.

If children have been encouraged to explore paint, they will have a variety of colors, marks, and shapes that they can call upon to express their idea. Refrain from making suggestions, telling them what to do, or how to do it. Instead, ask them to think about their options, how they will change the properties of paint so that they can use it to show what they have in mind (see pages 44, 48, 52, 53). If you notice they are 'drawing' in paint (outlining and filling in), remind them what they have learned

about using the brush to show a whole shape. Help them to trust the process.

Step #4:
Help them get started.

You should understand that a blank piece of paper can be intimidating and even self confident painters may need help organizing their plan of action (see pages 45, 49, 54). Ask them the obvious questions, "What will you do first, or, How will you hold your paper?" This breaks the task down into a manageable, tangible, first step. They can do something (mix a color, make a mark) and react to what they have done. The groundwork has been laid. They have an idea and have already begun to think about how to change the paint to represent that idea.

Talking with Kids

Painting is a visual language. To trust their own artistic instincts, children need verbal reassurance that they have successfully communicated their ideas. Inevitably, children will ask you to respond to their work, but it is not always clear what to say. Beginning painters, or younger ones, may or may not intend to represent something. No one wants to make the mistake of hurting a child's feelings by not recognizing something in his or her painting.

Using Erica's painting as a reference, here are some tips on how to talk to children about their paintings (see page 56). Erica was asked, *"What did you get better at doing over the summer vacation?"*

"Tell me about your painting."

The natural tendency is to respond with a compliment such as, "This is so beautiful!" However, this comment would mean little to Erica who is not particularly concerned with the aesthetic impact of her wave. Even though she has not included herself in the painting, she wants to show the exhilaration of playing in the surf. Instead ask Erica to, "Tell me about your painting," so you can discover clues about the associations she is making between the idea and the material. I do not advise you to ask her, "What is this?" because you may miss the point that she is as interested in showing how it feels to be tossed around in the wave as she is with showing what the wave actually looks like.

You can never go wrong describing what you see.

Descriptive comments indicate that you have looked carefully at the painting and taken the painter seriously. If you are not sure that Erica's image represents a wave you could say, "I see you have made a solid area with many layers of blues and greens, and on top are brushy, dancing lines." Your comment refers to how she has changed the paint (mixed several different blues and greens) and arranged it on the paper (applied it thick in one area, thin in another). Chances are that is all you will need to say, and she will happily tell you the rest of the story.

However, if you have heard her talking about riding the waves while she was painting, your comments can refer directly to her use of symbols (the arc shape to indicate a wave) and composition (the contrasting quality of the brushwork on the top edge). For example, you might say, "I see you have shown the way waves curl and it even looks like a foamy splash on the top."

One last important tip.

Beginning painters are finding their way, literally and figuratively. If they are to become confident, skilled painters, they must make this journey on their own. It takes a leap of faith to trust that the material will show them the way, and they need your support and encouragement. Applaud the fearless way children use their brush to show the speed of a horse at full canter. Marvel at the match they made between a color and the coziness of a campfire. Above all, don't forget to listen to what they have to say. As they talk about their work, you will get to know a side of your children and students that will delight and astound you.

This book began by explaining the double meaning of its title to young readers. Like Patrick they can be in the painted part of the basketball court. Or, they can be physically in the paint, exploring and discovering what it can do. After reading this section you may see a third meaning. For children to give shape to their ideas they must learn to work honestly in the material. Help them to think, feel, and imagine their experience *in the paint.*

Oh, and make sure there's lots of room on your refrigerator.

Acknowledgments

by Linda L. Louis

Heartfelt thanks to friends and colleagues Anne Lockwood, Lois Lord, Linda Melamid, Dina Petrillo, Andy Robinson, and Rina Shere, who read early drafts of this manuscript. Your knowledge of children, teaching, and the artistic process helped me to sort through what I saw clearly and what I needed to look at more closely. There is a long list of art education scholars whose work has influenced me, including the late Nancy Smith, and especially Judith Burton, whose insights on art and human development have guided my practice and inspired these pages. Thanks to Joan Cear and Susan Costello for editorial advice, to Celia Fuller for her creative design, to Owen Dugan for editing the manuscript, and to Hope Koturo for overseeing the production: you showed me "the ropes" while showing me respect. Lastly, many thanks to the talented art teachers who sent me the breathtaking artwork contained in these pages. Your efforts *in the paint* everyday keep our schools a place of possibilities for children.

Sheyda Ardalan, South Elementary School,
   New Canaan, CT
Dana Buck, Waterville Valley Elementary School,
   Waterville Valley, NH
Peggy Chambers, Thomson Elementary School,
   Washington, DC
Melissa Chang, Bank Street School for Children,
   New York, NY
Peggy Clark, Lincoln Elementary School,
   Melrose, MA

Bonnie Henderson, Center Elementary School,
   Hanover, MA
Karin Dando, The Multi-aged School (School 16),
   Yonkers, NY
Tracy Edlitz, The Scholastic Academy (School 18),
   Yonkers, NY
Sandy Edmonds, Daniel Webster Elementary School,
   New Rochelle, NY
Jennifer Eisenheim, Alcott School, Concord, MA
Elise Engler, P.S. 165 (Studio-In-A-School),
   New York, NY
Melanie Fisher, P.S. 158, New York, NY
Edith Gwathmey, Bank Street School for Children,
   New York, NY
Jean Patrick Icant-Pierre, Harlem School for the Arts,
   New York, NY
Phillip D. Kautz, P.S. 122 (Studio-In-A-School),
   New York, NY
Stephanie Liebowitz, P.S. 9, New York, NY
Lois Lord, Follow Through Program of Bank Street
   College of Education, at Fall River Public Schools,
   Fall River, MA
Mary Mayo, Ethical Culture School, New York, NY
Liza McLaughlin, Ethical Culture School, New York, NY
Nancy Beal Mostow, Village Community School,
   New York, NY
Suzanne Prodanas, B. B. Russell & Belmont
   Street Elementary Schools, Brockton, MA

A special thanks to my own students at the Village Community School in New York City.

Index

Photography Credits

Sources of photographs are as follows (numerals refer to pages):
Copyright © Bill Bytsura: back cover (bottom), 8.
Copyright © Paula Court: back flap (right), 35.
Copyright © Glenn James/NBA Photos: 19 (left).
Copyright © Roger Miller: front cover, back flap (left), 2, 3, 11, 12, 13, 14 (right, top and bottom), 15, 21 (center and right), 33, 34.
Bill Orcutt: back cover (top and middle), 10, 16, 17, 18, 19 (right), 20, 21 (left), 22, 23, 24 (right), 25, 26, 27 (top), 28, 29, 30, 31 (right), 32, 36, 37, 38 (right), 39, 40 (right), 41, 42 (right), 43, 44, 45, 46, 47, 48 (left), 49, 50, 51, 52, 53, 54, 55 (right), 56.
Copyright © Nora Trotman/NBA Photos: 7, 14 (bottom left), 24 (bottom left), 27 (bottom left), 31 (bottom left), 38 (bottom left), 40 (bottom left), 42 (bottom left), 48 (bottom right), 55 (left).
Copyright © Discover Financial Services, a division of NOVUS Services, Inc.: front flap (bottom), 8 (top right).

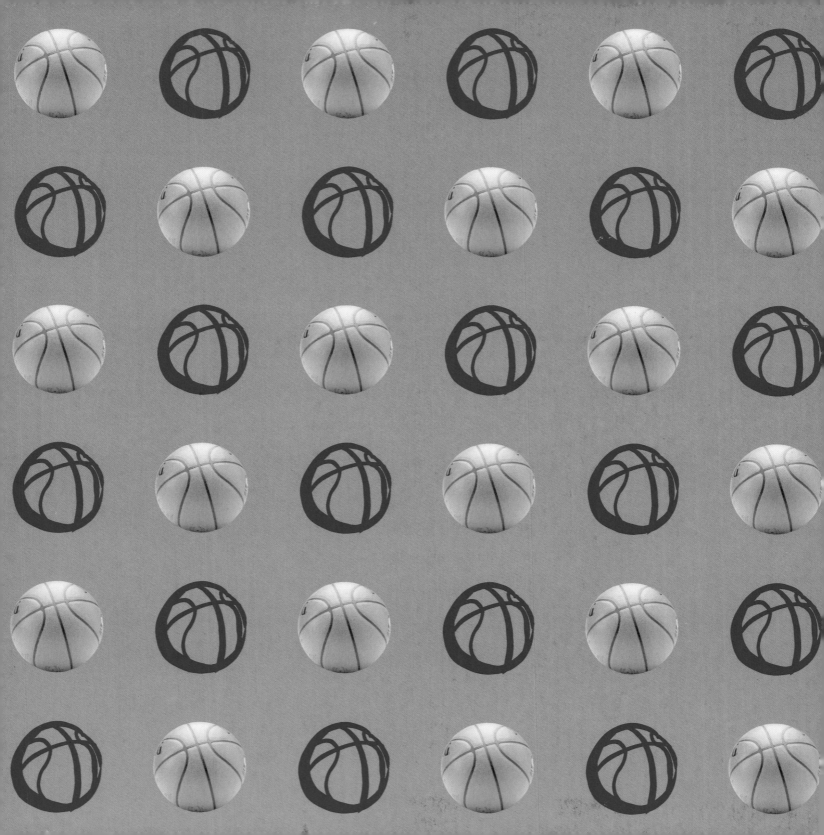